United States Presidents

Benjamin Harrison

Paul Joseph
ABDO Publishing Company

visit us at
www.abdopub.com

Published by ABDO Publishing Company, 4940 Viking Drive, Edina, Minnesota 55435.
Copyright © 2000 by Abdo Consulting Group, Inc. International copyrights reserved in
all countries. No part of this book may be reproduced in any form without written
permission from the publisher.

Published 2000
Printed in the United States of America.
Second printing 2002

Cover and Interior Photo credits: Archive Photos, UPI/Corbis-Bettmann

Contributing editors: Robert Italia, Tamara L. Britton, K.M. Brielmaier, Kate A. Furlong

Library of Congress Cataloging-in-Publication Data

Joseph, Paul, 1970-
    Benjamin Harrison / Paul Joseph.
        p. cm. -- (United States presidents)
    Includes index.
    Summary: Discusses the private life and political career of the
    grandson of the ninth president of the United States who was elected
    to be the twenty-third president in 1888.
        ISBN 1-57765-243-6
        1. Harrison, Benjamin, 1833-1901--Juvenile literature.
    2. Presidents--United States--Biography--Juvenile literature.
    [1. Harrison, Benjamin, 1833-1901. 2. Presidents.] I. Title.
    II. Series: United States presidents (Edina, Minn.)
    E702.J67 1999
    973.8'6'092--dc21
        [B]   98-17467
                                                         CIP
                                                          AC

Revised Edition 2002

Contents

Benjamin Harrison

*B*enjamin Harrison came from a long line of American leaders. Harrison was named after his great-grandfather, who signed the Declaration of Independence in 1776.

Harrison's grandfather was William Henry Harrison. He was a military hero who later became the ninth president.

Benjamin Harrison became a lawyer. He fought in the **Civil War**, and was a United States senator.

In 1889, Benjamin Harrison was sworn in as the twenty-third president of the United States.

Opposite page:
Benjamin Harrison

Benjamin Harrison (1833-1901)
Twenty-third President

BORN:	August 20, 1833
PLACE OF BIRTH:	North Bend, Ohio
ANCESTRY:	English
FATHER:	John Scott Harrison (1804-1878)
MOTHER:	Elizabeth Irwin Harrison (1810-1850)
WIVES:	First wife: Caroline "Carrie" Scott (1832-1892)
	Second wife: Mary Dimmick (1858-1948)
CHILDREN:	First wife: one boy, one girl
	Second wife: one girl
EDUCATION:	Private tutors, Cary's Academy,
	Miami University (Ohio)
RELIGION:	Presbyterian
OCCUPATION:	Lawyer, soldier
MILITARY SERVICE:	Appointed colonel of the Seventieth Indiana
	Volunteers in 1862, appointed brigadier general
	in 1865

POLITICAL PARTY: Republican

OFFICES HELD: Commissioner for the Court of Claims, city
                         attorney, state supreme court reporter of
                         Indiana, secretary of Indiana Republican State
                         Central Committee, U.S. senator

AGE AT INAUGURATION: 55

YEARS SERVED: 1889-1893

VICE PRESIDENT: Levi P. Morton

DIED: March 13, 1901, Indianapolis, Indiana, age 67

CAUSE OF DEATH: Natural causes

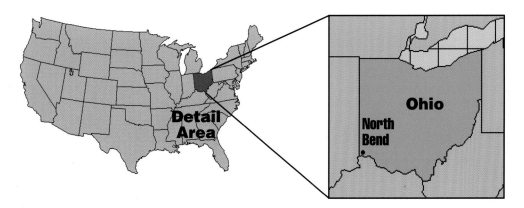

Birthplace of Benjamin Harrison

Young Ben

*B*enjamin Harrison was born in North Bend, Ohio, on August 20, 1833. Benjamin was the second son of John Scott Harrison and Elizabeth Irwin Harrison.

When Ben was just seven years old, his grandfather William Henry Harrison became president. The family was very happy and proud of him. Sadly, President Harrison died just one month after his **inauguration**.

John Scott and Elizabeth had eleven children. The children went

William Henry Harrison

8

to school at home. They had **tutors** so they would have a good education. Ben was an excellent student.

Ben liked to swim in the river, fish, and hunt. Ben also did chores such as cutting wood and carrying water home for cooking and drinking.

When Ben was fourteen years old, he went to college at Cary's Academy, near Cincinnati. In his third year of college, he transferred to Miami University in Oxford, Ohio. He was in love with Caroline Lavinia Scott, known as Carrie, who had moved to Oxford.

In college, Ben excelled in his studies and in debating. He gave wonderful speeches and loved getting up in front of a crowd. Ben graduated fourth in his class in 1852.

Family Man and Lawyer

*A*fter graduating from college, Harrison moved to Cincinnati to study law. In 1853, he married Carrie and they moved to Indianapolis, Indiana.

Harrison opened his own law office in Indianapolis. His business grew slowly. Harrison needed to earn more money. He took a job as a **court crier**. It paid $2.50 a day.

In 1855, Harrison took a law partner, William Wallace. They formed the Wallace and Harrison law firm. They enjoyed some success.

The Harrisons had their first child, Russell, in 1854. Their second child, Mary, was born in 1858. The Harrisons had a third child in 1861, but the baby died at birth. Harrison worked hard to support his family. Carrie stayed home with the children and volunteered at church.

During this time the country was divided over slavery. Harrison was against slavery. In 1856, he joined the **Republican** party. The Republicans opposed slavery.

In 1857, Harrison was elected city attorney of Indianapolis. In 1860, he was elected reporter of the Indiana Supreme Court. Harrison also continued to work at his law business to earn extra money.

Caroline Harrison

Civil War and Politics

*T*he **Civil War** began in 1861. The Northern states wanted to end slavery. The Southern states wanted to keep slavery. The South decided to leave the Union and form a new country. They called it the **Confederate States of America**.

On July 1, 1862, President Abraham Lincoln called for volunteers to fight in the war. Harrison bought a military cap and put a U.S. flag outside his office window. There, he **recruited** many soldiers.

Harrison became a colonel. During the day, he trained his men. At night, he studied military **strategy**. He always looked after his soldiers and was well liked. Because Harrison was short, his men called him "Little Ben."

In the summer of 1864, Harrison led his soldiers to Georgia. There, they fought many battles. Harrison took part in General Sherman's attack on Atlanta. He also fought heroically at nearby Peach Tree Creek. In 1865, President Lincoln made Harrison a **brigadier general**.

After the war ended in 1865, Harrison resumed his law practice. Because Harrison was a war hero, the **Republican** party thought that he would make a good candidate for political office. In 1876, Harrison began his career in politics.

Benjamin Harrison as a Civil War general

The Making of the Twenty-third United States President

1833
Born
August 20
in North
Bend, Ohio

1847
Attends
Cary's
Academy

1850
Transfers to
Miami
University
of Ohio

1852
Graduates
from college

1860
Elected reporter
of Indiana
Supreme Court

1861
Civil War
begins

1862
Recruits men for
Civil War;
becomes colonel
in 70th Indiana
Volunteers

1864
Leads
soldiers to
battle in
Georgia

1886
Loses re-
election for
senator

1888
Elected
president of the
United States

1890
Passes
important bills,
including
McKinley Tariff
Act

1892
Wife Caroline
dies; Grover
Cleveland
elected president

PRESIDENTIAL YEARS

Benjamin Harrison

"Let those who would die for the flag on the field of battle give a better proof of their patriotism and a higher glory to their country by promoting fraternity and justice."

1853 Marries Caroline Lavinia Scott; moves to Indianapolis, Indiana

1856 Joins the Republican party

1857 Elected city attorney of Indianapolis

1865 Civil War ends; Harrison discharged as brigadier general

1876 Runs for governor of Indiana but loses

1880 Elected U.S. senator

1893 Returns home to Indiana

1896 Marries Mary Dimmick

1901 Dies on March 13

Historic Events
during Harrison's Presidency

Electric automobile invented by William Morrison

Color photography invented by Frederic E. Ives

Doctors at Johns Hopkins Hospital in Maryland are first to use rubber gloves during surgery

Senator Harrison

*I*n 1876, the **Republicans** chose Harrison to run for governor of Indiana. Though he lost the election, his campaign brought him national attention. In 1879, President Rutherford B. Hayes appointed Harrison to the Mississippi River Commission.

Harrison was elected to the U.S. Senate in 1880. He and his family moved to Washington, D.C. Harrison soon became known as a good speaker and writer. He supported **civil service** reform and railroad **regulation**. He also worked hard for African American rights.

Harrison was popular among the former military men. He supported many **pension** bills for military veterans. These laws required the U.S. government to give money to people who had fought in wars.

Benjamin Harrison served in the Senate for six years. In 1886, he lost his re-election. His political career seemed over. He decided to return to Indiana and his law business.

Benjamin Harrison with his daughter and grandson

The Election of 1888

*I*n 1888, **Democratic** President Grover Cleveland ran for re-election. The **Republicans** chose Benjamin Harrison. His experience and speaking abilities made him a good candidate. The Republicans chose New York banker Levi P. Morton to run for vice president.

The election was very close. President Cleveland had 90,000 more popular votes than Harrison. But Harrison had 233 **electoral** votes to Cleveland's 168.

According to the U.S. Constitution, the president is elected by the electoral college and not by the popular vote. So, Harrison won the election. It was one of the few times in U.S. history that a president was elected without winning the popular vote. Benjamin Harrison was **inaugurated** on March 4, 1889.

Electoral Votes, 1888

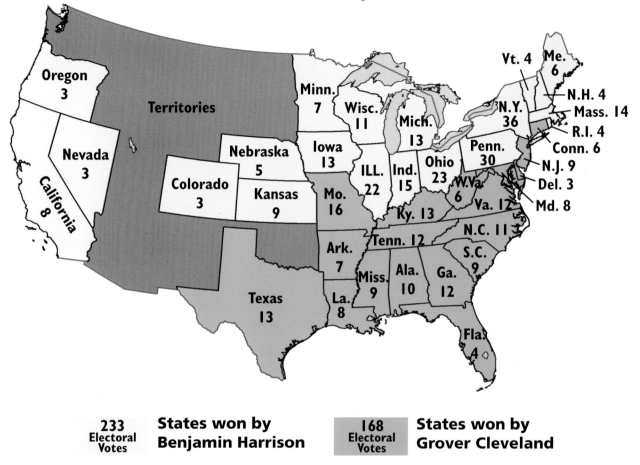

| 233 Electoral Votes | States won by Benjamin Harrison |
| 168 Electoral Votes | States won by Grover Cleveland |

Each state has electoral votes equal to the number of representatives it has in Congress. The state's population determines its number of representatives. States with large populations get more electoral votes.

When a candidate wins a state's popular vote, he or she wins its electoral votes. Grover Cleveland won more popular votes than Benjamin Harrison. But the states that Harrison won had more electoral votes. So, Harrison won the 1888 election.

The Twenty-third President

*T*he first Pan-American Conference was held in Washington, D.C., in 1889. President Harrison helped create trade agreements between the U.S. and Latin American countries.

In 1890, President Harrison approved four important bills. The first bill was the Dependent **Pension** Act. Some soldiers who fought in the **Civil War** were badly hurt. They could not work anymore. This new law gave these soldiers money to support their families.

The second bill was the Sherman Antitrust Act. Before 1890, it was possible for one U.S. company to control a certain market.

For example, one U.S. oil company could buy all the other oil companies. Then it could charge high prices for its oil. Americans would have to

The Sherman Antitrust Act and the Sherman Silver Purchase Act were named after Senator John Sherman.

pay these high prices because there would be no other place to buy oil. This is called a **trust** or **monopoly**. The Sherman Antitrust Act stopped this from happening.

The third bill was the Sherman Silver Purchase Act. Before this law was passed, U.S. money represented the gold supply kept at the U.S. Bullion Depository in Fort Knox, Kentucky. There was only as much money as there was gold.

Some people wanted more money printed. They said the nation's money could be represented by silver, too. The Sherman Silver Purchase Act allowed the government to use silver to represent money. Then it could print more money for people to use.

The fourth bill was the McKinley Tariff Act. This law placed high **tariffs** on products from other countries. Consumers did not like this new law. The added taxes made **foreign** goods

The McKinley Tariff Act was named after Congressman William McKinley.

more expensive. But the law was good for American businesses. People bought American goods because they cost less.

During Harrison's presidency, six new states joined the Union. They were: North and South Dakota, Montana, Washington, Wyoming, and Idaho. Also, Oklahoma Territory was opened for settlement in 1889. Before then Oklahoma was reserved for Native Americans to live in.

In 1892, President Harrison decided to run for re-election. Although he was making important gains for the country, some people still did not like him. The **Democrats** thought this was an opportunity to defeat **Republican** Harrison. They nominated former president Grover Cleveland.

Grover Cleveland

The United States during Benjamin Harrison's presidency

The Seven "Hats" of the U.S. President

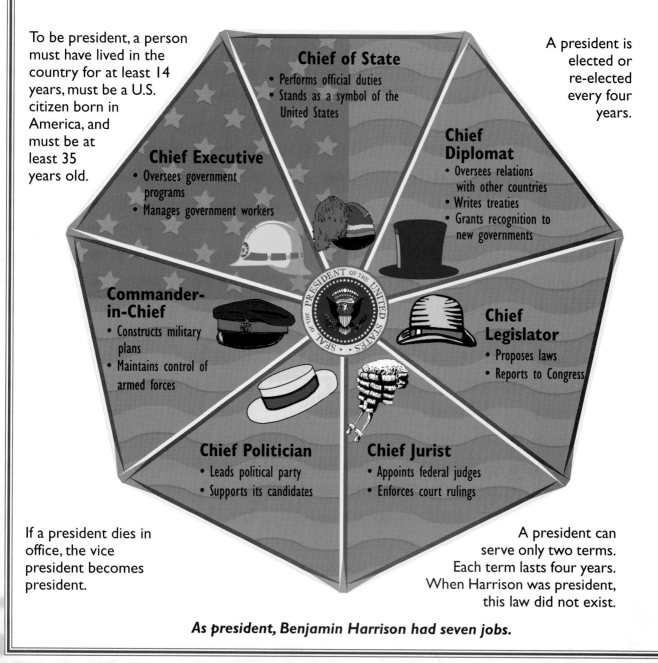

To be president, a person must have lived in the country for at least 14 years, must be a U.S. citizen born in America, and must be at least 35 years old.

A president is elected or re-elected every four years.

Chief of State
- Performs official duties
- Stands as a symbol of the United States

Chief Executive
- Oversees government programs
- Manages government workers

Chief Diplomat
- Oversees relations with other countries
- Writes treaties
- Grants recognition to new governments

Commander-in-Chief
- Constructs military plans
- Maintains control of armed forces

Chief Legislator
- Proposes laws
- Reports to Congress

Chief Politician
- Leads political party
- Supports its candidates

Chief Jurist
- Appoints federal judges
- Enforces court rulings

If a president dies in office, the vice president becomes president.

A president can serve only two terms. Each term lasts four years. When Harrison was president, this law did not exist.

As president, Benjamin Harrison had seven jobs.

The Three Branches of the U.S. Government

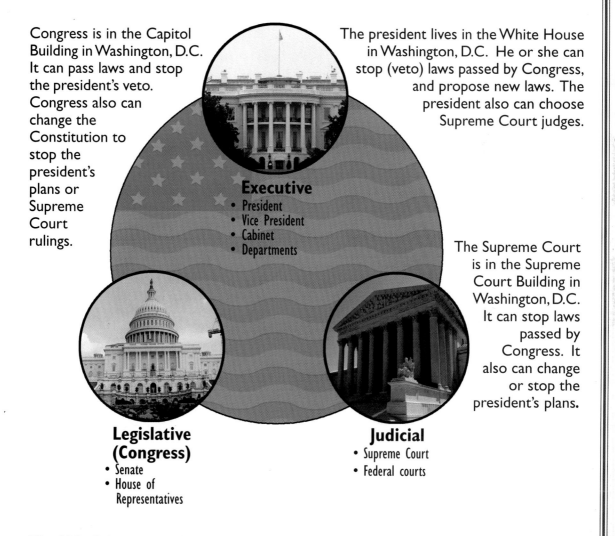

Congress is in the Capitol Building in Washington, D.C. It can pass laws and stop the president's veto. Congress also can change the Constitution to stop the president's plans or Supreme Court rulings.

The president lives in the White House in Washington, D.C. He or she can stop (veto) laws passed by Congress, and propose new laws. The president also can choose Supreme Court judges.

Executive
- President
- Vice President
- Cabinet
- Departments

The Supreme Court is in the Supreme Court Building in Washington, D.C. It can stop laws passed by Congress. It also can change or stop the president's plans.

Legislative (Congress)
- Senate
- House of Representatives

Judicial
- Supreme Court
- Federal courts

The U.S. Constitution formed three government branches. Each branch has power over the others. So, no single group or person can control the country. The Constitution calls this "separation of powers."

After the White House

*I*n 1892, tragedy struck the Harrison family. On October 25, Caroline Harrison died after a long illness. Eleven days later, President Harrison lost the election.

Harrison returned to his home in Indiana in March 1893. He practiced law and wrote for magazines. In 1897, Harrison also published a book on the **federal** government, titled *This Country of Ours.*

In 1896, Harrison married Mary Dimmick. Mary was Caroline's niece. She had lived in the White House and helped take care of the dying first lady. In 1897, Benjamin and Mary had a daughter named Elizabeth.

Benjamin Harrison lived another four years. He died on March 13, 1901. He is buried in Indianapolis beside his first wife.

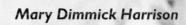
Mary Dimmick Harrison

Fun Facts

- Benjamin and William Harrison are the only grandfather and grandson in the history of the United States to both become president.

- The Harrisons had eleven family members living in the White House, but there was only one bathroom.

- During Benjamin Harrison's stay in the White House, a rat-catcher had to be hired because there were so many rats.

- Benjamin Harrison started the custom of flying the United States flag from public buildings.

- First Lady Caroline Harrison began the White House china collection. Every presidential family since has added to it.

- The Harrisons were the first family to have electricity in the White House. However, they were afraid of getting shocked when they touched the light switches. So, they hired an electrician to turn the White House lights on and off.

An illustration of Benjamin Harrison

Glossary

brigadier general - a one-star general.

civil service - the part of the government that runs matters not covered by the military, the courts, or laws.

Civil War - a war between the Union and the Confederate States of America from 1861 to 1865.

Confederate States of America - the eleven southern states that left the Union between 1860 and 1861.

court crier - a court official who shouts out announcements.

Democrat - a political party. When Harrison was president, they supported farmers and landowners.

electoral college - the group that formally elects the president and vice president by casting electoral votes. When people vote for president, the political party that gets the most votes in each state sends its representatives to the electoral college. There, they vote for their party's candidate.

federal - the central government of the United States.

foreign - from outside the United States.

inauguration - when someone is sworn into a political office.

monopoly - the complete control of a product or service.

pension - money paid by the government as a reward for military service.

recruit - to gather people together for a task.

regulation - when something is organized and governed.

Republican - a political party. When Harrison was president, they supported business and strong government.

strategy - a plan for battle.

tariff - a list of fees or taxes.

trust - a group of people or companies that control a product or service.

tutor - a private teacher.

Internet Sites

United States Presidents Information Page
http://historyoftheworld.com/soquel/prez.htm
Links to information about United States presidents. This site is very informative, with biographies on every president as well as speeches and debates, and other links.

The Presidents of the United States of America
http://www.whitehouse.gov/WH/glimpse/presidents/html/presidents.html
This site is from the White House. With an introduction from President Bill Clinton and biographies that include each president's inaugural address, this site is excellent. Get information on White House history, art in the White House, first ladies, first families, and much more.

POTUS—Presidents of the United States
http://www.ipl.org/ref/POTUS/
In this resource you will find background information, election results, cabinet members, presidency highlights, and some odd facts on each of the presidents. Links to biographies, historical documents, audio and video files, and other presidential sites are also included to enrich this site.

These sites are subject to change. Go to your favorite search engine and type in United States presidents for more sites.

Pass It On

History enthusiasts: educate readers around the country by passing on information you've learned about presidents or other important people who've changed history. Share your little-known facts and interesting stories. We want to hear from you!

To get posted on the ABDO Publishing Company Web site, email us at:
history@abdopub.com
Visit the ABDO Publishing Company Web site at www.abdopub.com

Index